POEMS BY MARY ROGERS-GRANTHAM

# Clear Velvet

Clear Velvet by Mary Rogers-Grantham
Copyright © 2015 by Mary Rogers-Grantham

Cover design and layout by Janelle Smith

Clear Velvet by Mary Rogers-Grantham
38p. ill. cm.
ISBN 978-0-9793362-1-8

---

All Rights Reserved. No part of this book may be reproduced, stored in a retrieval system, or transmitted in any form or by any means, electronic, mechanical, photocopying, recording, or otherwise, without permission in writing from MRK Publishing

MRK Publishing
PO Box 353431
Palm Coast, FL 32135-3431

**Printed in the United States of America**

For my sister Pearl, (cover photo), who passed away

December 2007

Table of Contents

| | |
|---|---|
| Amen Pews | 1 |
| Narratives | 2 |
| An Hour to Rest | 3 |
| Jarrell to the low down low… | 4 |
| Morning Review | 5 |
| Elegy for Pearl | 6 |
| I Laughed My Belly into Jell-O | 7 |
| Mourning in Daydreams | 8 |
| Charlotte | 9 |
| Morning Artist | 11 |
| Precinct Improvisation | 13 |
| In Drab Rooms with Medicine Johns | 15 |
| Ballad of Uncle Al | 16 |
| Shepherd Balladeer | 18 |
| Canvas Moments | 19 |
| Silent Savor | 20 |
| Travel Swatches I-VI | 21 |
| Turkic Caravan Woman | 23 |
| Colorist Fantasy | 24 |
| Letter to Pearl | 25 |
| French Lace in Kansas City | 30 |
| Author Page | 31 |

**Amen Pews**

The only chorus that morning was the choir, which issued
its gospel version of the Prayer of Saint Francis
and two selections from the *Donnie McClurkin Songbook*.

Afterwards, Preacher walked to the podium,
greeted the parishioners, and prepared them
with scripture for Sunday Morning Epistle.

When Preacher let go of the title, Beatitudes
were suspended in the vast ceiling of chandeliers.
It wasn't one that made the *New York Times*

Best Sermons List. Some members made sure
their heads swayed neither left nor right,
so not to look in disagreement with Preacher.

Others made sure their heads didn't rock back
and forth, so not to look in agreement with Preacher.
The Sunday Morning Amen Chorale who always sat

in the My Pew sections and uttered unanimous Amens
were frozen in place. Preacher worked the Beatitudes
with an attitude of a seasoned drummer.

But the sanctuary was silent as the Dead Sea,
a perfect portrait for the cover of *Time* magazine.
Parishioners resembled anxious patients

sitting in eye exam chairs, only moving their eyeballs
when the optometrist insists: "Look straight ahead at my nose.
Look at my left ear. Now, look at my right."

Like comatose caricatures with invisible neck braces,
they reserved their Amens to spit out car windows
on their drive home. Preacher ended the message,

"Amen, pews."

**Narratives**

Eurika lumbers into the classroom, late again.
She disrobes her backpack, sits down
and pulls out her paragraph. It's about
her night job at Kansas City International
where she mops floors and cleans pee splattered
toilet stools. "I'm going to work at an animal shelter."

Madra chides Steven about not having his homework
assignment prepared. He laughs at her and says,
"Don't get your draws tied up in a knot.
Why are you so concerned about it?
It's just a paragraph."

Julie writes about spending a weekend
with her boyfriend followed by a brawl
with her mother —who thought Julie
was hanging out at her girlfriend's house.
"My birthday weekend sucks.
I'm gonna be a mama."

Doffing writes about the time
a group of boys mugged him
for his bag of groceries, then
beat him bloody on a street in Cairo.
"I am grateful my family lives in Kansas City."

Zee missed school for the first
time this semester. Her email offers
an apology. The bathroom is home
because her three year old has diarrhea.
"I've attached my paragraph. It rocks"

**An Hour to Rest**

"Let's talk about Viola's relationship with her son, an alcoholic,
who in her words is 'a horse who doesn't carry his own weight.'"
—from *A Day Late and a Dollar Short* by Terry McMillan

Miricah lays her head on her desk.
Miricah falls asleep.
Old wounds.

His sluggish Stacy Adams slide and stumble.
Her brother Stelton's silhouette ambles to her bed.
His naked, weight crushes her.
His whispers are whiskey come-ons.
His salty hand covers her screams.


Miricah opens her eyes for a moment.
Miricah falls asleep.
Old wounds.

**Jarrell to the low down low…**

Jarrell exits the men's room down the hall.
He is breaking one of the school's dress codes,
totally, flaunting low down low with a purpose.

His unintentional intentional swagger dictates
how far he can lean and fake a left step forward,
and then, a slight lift and wide slide, a right foot

duet that helps the bottom of his booty hold fast
to a pair of faded jazzy jeans laced in leather.
A long sleeved pastel blue shirt buttoned

to the torso boasts a taut saddle brown waist
wrapped with elastic that bails out a surplus
of vibrant colored fabric —a pair of boxer shorts.

He rocks and swaggers and rocks. He's the mirage
of a defective two-step, scrambled. In my mind,
I sing a few lines from an R. Kelly tune, "Happy People."

"Step to the left. Step to the right. Spin around
and bring it down tonight". He rocks and swaggers
and rocks. Can't get a stepper's groove from that move.

Jarrell is a master of the art, low down low
wearing pants down low. At the door we nod hello.
I turn away, and he gets dressed.

**Morning Review**

He walks into the waiting room looking forward to his first therapy
since surgery. A Mission Easy Chair sits on the east corner wall
flanked by three sunlit colossal windows. He picks up *Morning Review*
and sits down. "Courageous woman," he thinks out loud.
"This time she's gone rogue."
A flock of women swarm the room.

*My son skis; not as much since he got married.*
*He used to ski all the time when he was in high school and college.*
*Wonder what the meaning behind that picture of Santa is.*
*I don't know. It's there every year. Looks like a Rockwell painting.*

Count the women invading his silence.
Count the skiers at the bunny slope.
Count the sun's rays at twilight.

*What does that sign on the door say?*
*No Cell Phones Allowed in Exercise Area, Please.*
*I guess they've had some kind of problems*
*with people talking on cell phones.*
*Well, there are other considerations,*
*like hospital equipment.*

Count the psychedelic cell phones in North America.
Count the Rockwell painting look-alikes in the world.
Count the cars in the mile wide parking lot.

He puts the *Morning Review* back on the table.
Garfield, Beetle Bailey, and Hagar the Horrible have to wait.

Count the women in the waiting room.
Count the green tea bags in the basket.
Count the octagonal tiles in the floor.

**Elegy for Pearl**
— *"For everything there is a season…"* (Ecclesiastes 3:1)

Her memorial service was over. We walked
out of the church at four in the afternoon.
A light mist, a brilliant sun and mourners
embraced us —sobering reminders
of our loved one, whose voice
would no longer kindle the hearth

of our lives. Somber faced chauffeurs
stood by opened doors, invited the family
inside gleaming black limousines. We sat down,
stared and waited. The sleek black hearse
ahead of us would lead the cavalcade
of cars wearing beads of headlights.

We passed the school grounds, the fairgrounds,
and Yark-Ghary's car lot. We passed mom and pop
stores heaving the aroma of Southern Sunset coffee
out their doors and through their windows. We passed
black Angus grazing in fields littered with loose saffron
colored grass in dense pasture lands.

The only expression was the driver's eyes darting
about the rearview mirror from one family member
to the other. Just beyond Capp Murray Bend
the cemetery came into full view. Like a blue print
on a plot of earth, grave markers and headstones
in formation —a layout for loved ones.

**I Laughed My Belly into Jell-O**

I stood in the doorway.

The ceiling fan turned slowly beneath
the light bulb, sending shivering glows
around the room like the last embers
of a campfire.

I entered your room.

One butterscotch left in cellophane
lay on your dresser. I remembered
your high school acting debut
in the comedy, *The Devil's Funeral*,
while eating it. I laughed my belly
into Jell-O.

I closed the door behind me.

A faded orange overstuffed chair
sat next to the bed. I walked over
and sat in it. An 81/2 x 12 framed
caricature of you boasting a boisterous
grin defied my sigh. I heard you laugh.
I laughed my belly into Jell-O.

I got up from the overstuffed chair.

While walking the compass of your room,
I grinned back at the photo. Your presence
embraced me; your eyes dried my tears.
A box of tissues sat on top of the dresser.
I took one and then, left your room.

Through my tears,
I laughed my belly into Jell-O.

**Mourning in Daydreams**

She wants to

watch you check
her out from shoes to hair,
then hear you say,
You're looking real fine, today

see you sitting in your chocolate
corduroy chair, rocking
back and forth while reading
*Jet* magazine

inhale smooth Gevalia mingled
with zesty chittlin vapors
in your pine wood kitchen
on Thanksgiving morning

taste your southern deep-fried
chicken and succulent garlic
meatloaf that could shut down
any New Orleans kitchen

hear your tenor hum melt
into Johnnie Taylor's crooning
"Nothing's as Beautiful as You"
on the blues radio station.

She wants to laugh with you again,
until tears and bellies roll.

**Charlotte**
—after Anita Scott Coleman

Dolly, you flawless porcelain white girl
My aunt gave you to me
Drove you all the way from Texas to Arkansas
You rode in the trunk of her car
    inside a cardboard coffin.


You *are* quite the pretty one
Dressed up in lilac layers of nylon
I love you because you look like who I'd
    like to look like
I'd like to meet your maker.
I'd ask what he could do to make me
    look like you

You, with your glistening gold strands
Me, with my stubborn black locks

    Yet and still, I love God.

Warm blood runs through my veins
fertilizing my brazen black locks.
From a pound of man made white porcelain,
your empty sea blue glass eyes stare into mine

I wish we could exchange places, Dolly
So you'd know how it feels to wake up each day
   and discover you're still the same little colored girl.

**Morning Artist**

—after Dan Beachy-Quick

> aged in layers
> her hands like marionettes
> grip her victim
>
> this arctic morning
>
> the broom her companion
> head
> bowed to her task
> she
>
> sweeps the
> parking spaces and
> sidewalks//she is
>
> an old woman
> face full of
> storylines// each
>
> with its own
> setting in
> a
>
> geography of
> living //her life
> buried somewhere
> in her
> hollow
> cheeks//narratives
> go untold while
> she
>
> continues a task
> she knows by

heart//the monotonous
gravelly
sweeping sounds

on sidewalks and
parking spaces
rarely does she look
up

as cars drive into the parking lot
to occupy her spaces//rarely
does she

notice the drivers who

exit their cars and
travel her sidewalks
she asks
nothing //this artist of my mornings

no one seems
to notice her//maybe
she doesn't
mind

I notice her
"Morning!"

**Precinct Improvisation**

—after Richard Siken


I walk out the backdoor thinking my two-year-old black Lab, Hannah,

                                              is following me, but she

bolts ahead, mindless

   of the scandalous white ground cover and the unforgiving

snowfall. The yard

is bright, the flower bed is next to the weathered wooden

fence,

                              the book on the hearth is *A Christmas*

*Carol.*

This morning I'm thinking of the laughter inside paucity

at the Cratchit house and I stare at Hannah like I'm looking

through the night,

                                                  counting

snowflakes.

                                    She wants to pee, I can't

blame her for that,

and maybe a smile looks idiotic when it grows into a grin

    but she tells me

she loves this, she tells me she's not afraid.

                          She pees, she expects to

play.

        The snow-covered precinct. The white shawl

houses.

Draw a circle in the snow with your foot. Imagine a hike in the

Sedona Mountains.

                        Imagine tranquility. Imagine

sweat.

Drinking green tea inhibits cancer cell growth. Amen is an agreement with a convincing

part of a message. October snow shadows are the making of Easter bouquets.

**In Drab Rooms with Medicine Johns**

Neurologists attempted to liberate
me with their wit before sliding
inside their tunnel piped
with Bach's *Sarabande in A
Major*. The last request.

No soft saffron lighting to erase
my senses. I closed my eyes, then
dared the spirited harpsichord
to dull the pulse in the tunnel.

No warmed dusk scented oils
to anoint my body nor massage
my tension. I pretended the cold
lubricants made the jabs easier.

New Johns.
Drab rooms.
Hard cots.

I became a prostitute
 in a pool of inquiries.

Dazed eyes.
Muffled whispers.
Throbbing pain.

One week.
Two weeks.
Three months.
One year.

I took charge of my anatomy,
walked out of my last drab room,
and set myself free from cheerful medicine Johns,
their strange beds in colorless rooms.

**Ballad of Uncle Al**

Now, mind you, Mister didn't know
That Uncle Al was a midnight 'ho.'
Lean and lanky, with wavy hair
He pierced the nights without a dare
   without a dare
   without a dare
He pierced the nights without a dare


When one sultry summer morn
Five teen boys traveled to work a farm
From the bed of Mister's truck
Uncle Al became awestruck
   awestruck
   awestruck
Uncle Al became awestruck


In the distance, they could see
A red dress posed beside the tree
Where Mister usually parked his truck
And the teens stepped down, young buck by buck
   young buck by buck
   young buck by buck
And the teens stepped down, young buck by buck

Today, a young girl in a fire red dress
Gravely waited for her test

Mister's young daughter now in full view

Behind the fire red dress, her innocence peaked through

    peaked through

    peaked through

Behind the fire red dress, her innocence peaked through


He drove passed his daughter dressed like a "ho"

Uncle Al shaped his lips in the form of an O

The teen boys chided, "Al, No! No! No!"

But his long shrill whistle erased their echoes.

    "Al, No! No! No!"

    "Al, No! No! No!"

But his long shrill whistle erased their echoes.


From his rearview mirror, Mister witnessed the sight

Uncle Al's shrill whistle in broad daylight

The daughter in red screamed "I hope you rot in hell!"

Four teen boys went to work, and Uncle Al went to jail

    went to jail

    went to jail

Four teen boys went to work, and Uncle Al went to jail.

**Shepherd Balladeer**
*For Luther Vandross*
—after Gwendolyn Brooks

For a while

you sent

tender messages

to your flock.

They waited for

your meticulous lyrics,

your charming delivery

of "A House is Not a Home,"

"Dance With my Father, Again,"

and other narratives

encouraging endless love,

sincere and colossal,

we are products

of each other,

we are issues

of each other's.

For a while

you tendered them with ballads,

here and now.

**Canvas Moments**
*A Thomas Kincade Found Poem*


You can discover a world of warm yellows in glowing lights from within English cottages, modest chapels and brilliant cityscapes.

Warm yellows in glowing lights from rustic stone hearths and windows. His paintings project lambent lights and quiet retreats.

Rustic stone hearths find their places inside thatch roof hutches,
often escorted by the music of a gurgling creek and droning bees.

Thatch roof hutches nestled inside flowering foxglove and lilac shrubs,
overarching dogwood and eucalyptus trees layered like vases on display.

You are drawn to their graceful cobblestone paths, where earth peers between the brokenness. Like bathing in June breezes and

showering in July rain. You are drawn, then held captive in canvas
moments and timeless lights. Even canvas moments can allow soft

edges, a warm palette and a total sense of light. Golden saffron and poppy, bathed in gamboge, create warm yellows.

If only for a canvas moment, a foxglove cottage is home.

**Silent Savor**

The morning following Thanksgiving, Mimi is up at 6 a. m. I hear her bedroom door squeak open and shut; she keeps forgetting to put a drop of Bee Oil on the top hinge. I lay awake while she walks down the hallway and into the kitchen, her morning routine. It has been four months, but her belly still heaves every time she thinks of her first-born, dead at 42. I wonder what she'll eat this morning. I walk in and see her sitting at her table-for-two by the window, looking out on the lake, and eating a muddled meal of sliced beets on banana nut bread. I sit down and wait for the coffee to brew. She takes care not to leave anything on the plate, dragging each remaining crumb through juice the color of blood. I watch her carefully cull each breadcrumb into a miniature mass, making sure they get the red juice treatment before the last savor. Her heart hemorrhages. Our silence is humbling. I keep our silence company.

**Travel Swatches I-VI**
—after Audre Lorde
*I*
Bel-lah
I used to love our child's play laughter
that often found its way to the ears
of authority, just after pee had soaked
clear through my skirt.
We laughed hard,
and then we exhaled.
*II*
Shari
I heard your edgy blues
but got bored with the body politic
when deception defied confidence
my soul became restless
when your acts of allegiance
emanated sinister repression.
*III*
Haley
I admired your valor
to teach Black students.
I am sorry you exchanged
their academic needs
with your daughter stories.
They show up in college English
incompetent.
*IV*
Belinda
Restless, erotic spirit
I am sorry your insatiable river
crossed the state line,
rolled into smoke filled parlors,
barbershops and noonday blues rooms.
"Them that got…"

*V*
Joiss
rebel English teacher
extracted remarks from players like,
"She's a looker" and "Hey girl."
Your man had to be your age
 and boast "a hard back."
Prancing before your students and
strutting among your colleagues,
I watched you on both runways,
model Body Belligerent.
*VI*
Bonnie
I remember your Paul Laurence Dunbar
raspy recitations to your literature students.
In your baritone smoker's voice
you eloquently delivered "We Wear the Mask,"
then, your transition rendition in dialect
of "Po Lil' Lamb.
I admired your courageous
Angela Davis sermonettes.
I dreamed you were a Black Panther.

## Turkic Caravan Woman

*An Ancient Chinese Sculpture*

if there was a woman
whose skin was as gray as museum galleries
that now house and guard her                    if

there was a woman
who straddled linen layered humps
and traveled with camel caravans                if there

was a woman
who wore a lofty hat
and one-piece body suit draped in a tunic    if there was

a woman
who strong-armed an ancient beast
while her hungry child fed at her breast     if there was a

woman
with the courage to navigate a slow-witted creature
over sweltering dust drifted plains—

There was a Turkic Caravan Woman.

**Colorist Fantasy**

Topaz fruit resembling an old lace gourd,
floats lazily along a salty green swell.

Down by a bayou filled with cold sauvignon,
serpentine women bathe in long yellow grasses.

A colorist stirs the bayou at high noon,
bubbles blink and break against the sun.

Alice blue men gather under baobab trees,
and read narratives written on scrolls.

**Letter to Pearl**

—Kansas City, March 2008

Three months have passed since you went away. I've

cried my eyes dry. Each time I look out through swollen

eyelids, I ask God, why. Then I am reminded that you

are rejoicing at your family reunion with Mother and Daddy.

I smile.


I still dress "real fine" each day, whether I'm leaving

home or not, whether I feel good or not when I wake up each

morning.

You often spoke about my dress in your own complimentary

ways.

 "Merlee, I like your outfit. Where are you going today?"

 When I'd say, "Nowhere. Why?" You'd say,

"You're looking "real fine." I thought you were going

somewhere."

When you didn't speak of my dress, your eyes did. Like a road

map,

they started at my head and meticulously traveled to my feet.

You'd look away and begin to gently rock yourself back and forth.

It began to happen often enough that I took notice, and finally made meaning of it. It was your warm, voiceless compliment.

I carry on the tradition the four of us girls had, capturing meaningful and humorous sayings from our lovely little community. Like, Miss Willie Jeff,
our Sunday school teacher, who used to say, "I don't care whether I'm going somewhere or not. I don't care if I feel good or not. When I get up every morning, Willie Jeff is going to make herself look real fine." She would make this miniature speech whenever one of her students came into her class acting lethargic or looking abominable. I am reminded each morning of her words as I get out of bed and make myself look "real fine."

Soon after you left, I spent three days in the hospital. My doctor's diagnosis was grief stress. During the days I spent there, I reflected on the happy times we had together and the challenges we had to endure, but we had each other. After losing Mother and Daddy, we never grieved the way we should have grieved. I didn't know whether it was because we didn't know how to do so, or whether we adhered to society's tutorial: Hide your emotions, cry behind closed doors, take a few days off, and then resurface. Anyway, we got on with our life as best we could, as best we knew how. Today, I ask, "Who said?"

This time, I didn't emerge from grief in a few days. This time, I didn't adhere to society's grief tutorial. This time, someone greater than society captured my attention, and I listened. While I was hospitalized, waiting for my 2 gram sodium diet meals, potassium and antibiotic IVs, I was reminded of one of the most renown and effective steps program, Alcoholics Anonymous (AA). Initially used for alcoholics, research has proven it to be effective for non-alcoholics in various problematic areas. Step one: Admit you have a problem. Sister, I admitted that I had a problem. Mine was grief. My body heated up to a 103.8 temperature. My body cooled down to teeth chatters and body convulsions.

When I left the hospital, my doctor wrote a twelve-day script, unlike the lyrical twelve days of Christmas. Along with that, she ordered "Rest, rest and more rest." When I asked her how I could do that, especially with the semester starting in six days, she said, "Easy. You take a sabbatical or you take three daily doses of death." That convinced me.

I found a wonderful grief-sharing ministry and have spent six rewarding weeks with other grievers like me. We have cried together, blown our nose together, and shared activities together. We made beautiful collages, each representing the favorite things our loved ones enjoyed. Cutting out of magazines reminded me of the times we cut out our favorite paper dolls. I chose beautiful pictures that represented your favorite thing to do, cook. Wondrous cooking. Scrumpdilly-iscous cooking. Blackberry cobblers and peach cobblers with mouth watering flaky crusts. Making chow chow and canning it. Cornbread that Aunt Jemima would love.

We wrote an essay about our loved one that captured memories, including the time we spent with them while they

planned their departure from us. I was reminded of my anger about you leaving abruptly, not affording me the honor of being there with you as your journey came to a close. On the other hand, I could write about the precious memories, so I did and titled it "Home of a Lady Tiger." My narrative was packaged with laughter
and highlights of your basketball career. I said you could pamper a meal far beyond the great cooks and great cookbooks. Your southern fried chicken and meat loaf could shut down a New Orleans kitchen. Your pastries could be the delight of France. Your laughter could scale the Colorado Mountains.

So, now I write this letter and think of you. Good-bye is still inside the last jar
of canned apple jelly you left on the top shelf of your pantry.

**French Lace in Kansas City**

*Loose Park*

Virgin white petals dabbed
with anemic yellow hues,
turned the corner. Chipmunk rested
in their shadow. Lifting two front legs
and clasping its two paws —prayer like.
After appearing to serve a quick, clumsy bow
to fragrant French Lace roses, Chipmunk
scurried across the sidewalk to explore
more varieties in the Rose Garden.

A light, south wind moved through the foliage,
stirred it to a nod —up, then down.
    A few stray mists from the fountain
    settled on my forehead.

# About the Author

Mary Rogers-Grantham adores family and teaching, respects nature and humanity, and enjoys writing poetry and traveling. These subjects are often presented in poetic memoirs and in other poetic forms, which have been published in several literary journals. Her poetry collections include *It's Okay: Poetic Memoirs*, *Clear Velvet*, *Under a Daylight Moon*, and *Rotating Reflections: A Poetry Trio*. Mary grew up in Southwest Arkansas and taught high school and college English in Kansas City, Missouri. She is a new Florida resident, teaches at Flagler College in St. Augustine and is working on her next poetry collection *Turn Down the Sun*.

www.ingramcontent.com/pod-product-compliance
Lightning Source LLC
Chambersburg PA
CBHW050608300426
44112CB00013B/2134